Fact Finders®

The Story of the
American Revolution

The Rebellious Colonists and the Causes of the American Revolution

by Christopher Forest

Consultant:
Richard Bell
Assistant Professor, Department of History
University of Maryland
College Park, Maryland

CAPSTONE PRESS
a capstone imprint

Fact Finders are published by Capstone Press,
1710 Roe Crest Drive, North Mankato, Minnesota 56003.
www.capstonepub.com

Library of Congress Cataloging-in-Publication Data
Forest, Christopher.
The rebellious colonists and the causes of the American Revolution / by
Christopher Forest.
    p. cm. — (Fact finders. The story of the American Revolution)
Includes bibliographical references and index.
Summary: "Describes causes and events leading up to the Revolutionary
    War"—Provided by publisher.
ISBN 978-1-4296-8428-6 (library binding)
ISBN 978-1-4296-9290-8 (paperback)
ISBN 978-1-62065-243-5 (ebook PDF)
1. United States—History—Revolution, 1775–1783—Causes—Juvenile literature. I.
    Title.

E210.F67 2013
973.3'11—dc23   2011046679

Editorial Credits
Mari Bolte, editor; Heidi Thompson, designer; Wanda Winch, media researcher;
Laura Manthe, production specialist

Photo Credits
Alamy: Mary Evans Picture Library, 19, 27, North Wind Picture Archives, 10, 13,
17, 20, 23; The Bridgeman Art Library International: Yale Center for British Art/
Paul Mellon Collection, USA/William Clark (1808-1883), 12; Corbis: Bettmann,
7, Blue Lantern Studio/Laughing E, 11; Library of Congress: Prints and
Photographs Division, 16, 25; Shutterstock: Christophe Boisson, grunge stripe
design; SuperStock Inc: Pantheon, 14; U.S. Department of the Interior: National
Atlas of the United States, 1970, 9

Printed in the United States of America in Brainerd, Minnesota.
032012   006672BANGF12

Table of Contents

Direct quotations appear on the following pages:
Page 20, from *The Writings of Samuel Adams*, by Samuel Adams,
    collected and edited by Harry Alonzo Cushing (New York:
    G. P. Putnam's Sons, 1904–08.)

CHAPTER 1

Growing Tensions

The year 1763 brought big changes to America. British troops and American Indian tribes had just ended a war with the French. France's defeat gave Great Britain control of land east of the Mississippi River. The British also earned territories in India and the Caribbean.

However, the end of the war was the beginning of a new problem. Great Britain ruled 13 colonies in America. The colonies had thrived for 100 years and were growing. Colonists who lived there wanted to expand west. But Britain was overwhelmed with the reality of controlling that much space.

British Parliament began passing new laws to control the territories. The colonists felt the laws took away their rights. Angry colonists banded together to voice their concerns. British officials thought the colonists were unreasonable. Neither side could agree on what to do. Small problems grew into big ones. By April 1775, tensions between the two sides were at their highest. These disagreements ignited the American Revolution.

parliament: a group of people who make laws and run the government

The 13 Original Colonies

(part of Massachusetts)

N.H.

Lake Champlain

Fort Ticonderoga

Marblehead

New York

Mass. Boston

Hudson R.

Conn. R.I.

Pennsylvania

Philadelphia New Jersey

Maryland Delaware

St. Mary's City

Virginia

Chesapeake Bay

Jamestown

North Carolina

South Carolina

Georgia

Atlantic Ocean

New England Colonies
Middle Colonies
Southern Colonies

0   100   200 miles
0   100   200 kilometers

The 13 colonies were divided into the New England, Middle, and Southern colonies.

CHAPTER 2

The First Offenses

Two early events shaped the colonists' growing frustrations toward Great Britain. Both events involved Great Britain's control over the colonies. The colonists began to wonder whether members of Parliament had their best interests at heart.

The French and Indian War (1756–1763)

European countries had been exploring America since the 1500s. The French lived and traded with the American Indians. The British built colonies along the Atlantic coast. Both countries wanted to control the Ohio River Valley. Settling near the river would make travel and trade easy.

The two countries had fought over North America before. But this would be a deciding battle. The war lasted for more than seven years. Eventually Great Britain, with the help of its colonists, won. But the war had caused tension between Britain and the colonists.

Colonists wanted to fight for their home country. They asked for their own army. But their request was denied. Instead British troops were sent to the colonies. The British officers demanded that colonists supply food and housing for their soldiers.

In Europe, the French and Indian War was called the Seven Years' War.

Colonists dressed for battle were often turned away. Eventually they were allowed to fight, but they were often looked down upon by British officers as inferior fighters. Without their help, Great Britain might not have been victorious.

The war had been expensive. Great Britain was left with large debts. To pay these bills, the government decided to raise taxes on everything, including goods sent to the colonies. Some of the taxes restricted the colonists' everyday lives. Other taxes were costly or forced the colonists to rely on Great Britain for goods. The colonists felt the taxes were unfair and did not want to pay them.

debt: money that a person owes

The Proclamation of 1763

By winning the war, the British gained France's territory in America. Many American Indians who had fought for France lived on that land. The Indians worried that they would be punished for siding with France. Colonists and Indians had clashed before. And as colonists began moving west, Indians found it difficult to maintain their way of life.

To ease the tension between the Indians and colonists, Great Britain drew a boundary line. The boundary was called the Proclamation Line. The colonists were supposed to live east of this line. Land to the west was reserved for the American Indians.

Parliament hoped the line would limit the colonists to the coast. If the colonists moved too far inland, they might start making or growing their own goods. Then they would stop trading with Great Britain. Or colonists might start trading with other countries. British leaders believed limiting trade with other countries was one way to keep the colonists under control.

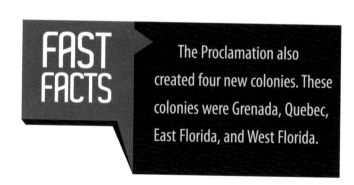

FAST FACTS

The Proclamation also created four new colonies. These colonies were Grenada, Quebec, East Florida, and West Florida.

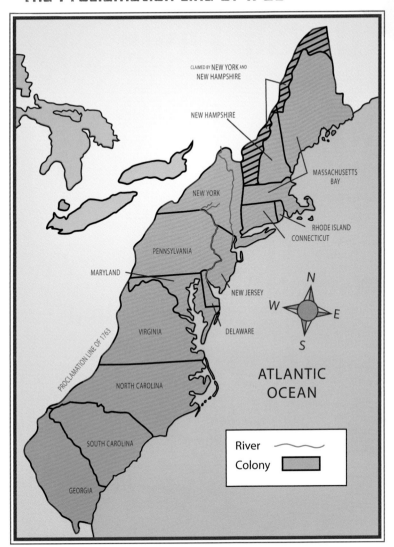

The Grenada colony was part of the Caribbean islands (not shown).

The colonists were disappointed and angry about the boundary. They had hoped to settle on the newly-gained territory. They also felt that, since they helped win the war, they should be able to enjoy the rewards. It was just the first of many criticisms the colonists would have against Great Britain.

CHAPTER 3

Unfair Laws

Relations between the colonists and Great Britain continued to decline after a series of laws and taxes were passed. Men who lived across the ocean wrote the laws for the colonies. These laws affected all aspects of the colonists' lives. The colonists paid British taxes but had no say in the government. Angry colonists began demanding:

"No taxation without representation!"

Some riots grew out of control as thousands of angry colonists marched together.

The Sugar Act (1764)

In an effort to pay war debts, Great Britain's Parliament passed the Sugar Act. This act actually reduced an existing tax on sugar and molasses by half. It was hoped that lowering the tax would encourage the colonists to pay the fee.

Before 1764 many merchants smuggled molasses into the colonies to avoid the tax. Smugglers who got caught were tried by American juries and usually let go. Under the Sugar Act, smugglers would be tried without juries by British courts. Those found guilty could have their entire shipload of goods confiscated.

Great Britain's taxes increased the price of goods brought into the colonies. More merchants began selling smuggled goods to keep their prices low.

smuggle: to bring something or someone into or out of a country illegally

confiscate: to take something by authority

Trade items from countries outside Great Britain were also taxed. And merchants were being told how certain products, such as lumber, should be traded.

Great Britain sent more ships to the colonies to put the acts into effect. Merchants protested. They didn't care if the tax had been lowered—they didn't want to pay it at all. They felt that the Sugar Act weakened the rum and lumber trades. Both were great moneymakers for the colonists.

The Sugar Act tried to reduce trade between the colonies and the Caribbean islands that weren't controlled by Great Britain.

The Quartering Act (1765)

After the French and Indian War, Great Britain sent 10,000 troops to the colonies. They were there to protect the colonies from the French. But the colonists didn't think they needed protection. The French were no longer a threat. Many felt the soldiers were there to frighten the colonists into obeying the new laws.

The soldiers needed a place to live. The Quartering Act was passed, forcing the colonists to provide housing for the soldiers. Colonists were often expected to provide food and beds too. The British didn't pay for these services, even when buildings and supplies were limited.

The sudden appearance of so many British soldiers made colonists afraid.

Colonists were not used to having soldiers in their towns and cities. They were also angry that they were forced to house the soldiers. They didn't want to pay for something they were forced into.

The Stamp Act (1765)

Before 1765 all merchants paid a tax on official papers. The paper was stamped to show the tax had been paid. Then another fund-raising act was passed—the Stamp Act.

Colonists opposed British soldiers bringing stamped paper to the colonies.

The Stamp Act forced colonists to pay a tax on every piece of paper they bought. Now everyday items, such as books and newspapers, were taxed too.

If colonists were allowed in Parliament, they might have argued against the Stamp and Sugar Acts. They might have changed the way British laws were written. Instead the colonists had no voice. They were forced to follow whatever laws Parliament passed.

The Sugar Act had affected only a small number of people. The Stamp Act, however, had a much greater reach. Angry protests were held. Mobs attacked British officials. They broke into British homes and set their possessions on fire. Men in charge of collecting the stamp tax quit their jobs out of fear. In 1766 the Stamp Act was repealed.

Both Sides of the Story

British citizens had to pay taxes after the French and Indian War too. They did not understand the colonists' anger over the Stamp Act. Great Britain had gone into great debt to protect the colonies. British citizens felt that colonists should help repay some of that debt.

repeal: to officially cancel something, such as a law

The Townshend Acts (1767)

In 1767 Parliament member Charles Townshend thought of another tax to raise money. He proposed placing taxes on items that were not made in the colonies, including paper, glass, tea, lead, and paint. These items were things that were hard to smuggle and would be easy to track. They could also only be bought from Great Britain.

Charles Townshend (1725–1767)

The Stamp Act had affected paper already in the colonies. Townshend thought that people had been upset over paying taxes on common items in the colonies. He believed they would not object to taxes on imported goods. Those items had not yet been brought into the colonies. But Townshend was wrong. Colonists opposed any new taxes.

The colonists felt the acts challenged their rights. Now anyone caught smuggling would face trial by British judges, not colonial juries. Homes and businesses could be searched for smuggled goods. Any suspected smuggled goods could be seized.

import: to bring goods into one country from another

16

Checking Cargo

In 1768 British officials took over two ships belonging to Patriot John Hancock. They claimed Hancock was involved with smuggling and not paying taxes. The charges were likely true. However, Hancock was a popular citizen in Boston. The accusations enraged the colonists. Angry mobs gathered throughout Boston during Hancock's trial. Eventually the charges were dropped.

The Townshend Acts were the final straw. These laws were the third new tax forced upon the colonists. They felt the acts limited business and trade. Boycotts took place on British goods. Parliament repealed most of the Townshend Acts in 1770. However, they kept the tax on tea.

The Townshend Acts allowed British officials to enter colonists' homes and search for smuggled items.

boycott: to refuse to take part in something as a way of making a protest

The Tea Act (1773)

In 1773 the East India Tea Company was in trouble. It was the primary tea company in Great Britain, but it was losing money. Colonists didn't want to pay taxes on British tea. To avoid the tax, they smuggled Dutch tea into the colonies. The company was left with warehouses full of unsold tea and growing debt.

The British government was afraid that the country's economy would suffer if the company went bankrupt. So Parliament passed the Tea Act. The government loaned the company money to ship tea to the colonies. Only the company's agents would be allowed to sell tea there. Agents would not have to pay taxes on the tea. The taxes would be paid by the colonists. The Tea Act would allow the company to sell its tea at a lower price than the smuggled Dutch tea.

Smuggling

The tax acts were one way Great Britain controlled trade in the colonies. Colonists were expected to buy and sell items chosen for them by Parliament. But the colonists could get around the laws by smuggling.

Ship captains chose routes that avoided British ships at sea. Merchants bribed British officials to look the other way as their ships unloaded Dutch, French, or Spanish goods. These smuggled goods were never officially recorded, so they were not taxed. It is estimated that goods worth more than 700,000 British pounds were smuggled into the colonies every year. That would be about $11 million in today's money.

Colonists opposed the act for several reasons. Some of their favorite teas came from other countries. Tea importers who obeyed the law but were not part of the company would be put out of business. And it was another tax forced upon them. Colonists vowed to boycott the tea.

The colonists refused to unload the East India tea when it arrived in Boston. Day after day passed, and the tea remained on the ship. It seemed that things were at a standstill. Colonists finally decided to take action. On December 16, 1773, they dumped all the tea into the harbor. The event became known as the Boston Tea Party.

Nobody was hurt during the Boston Tea Party. The Patriots' only goal was to destroy the tea.

The Intolerable Acts (1774)

In 1774 the government passed a series of laws called the Intolerable Acts. The acts were written to punish colonists for the Boston Tea Party. Although only a few had dumped the tea, everyone would be held responsible.

**It appears that we have been tried and condemned, and are to be punished ...
—Samuel Adams, May 14, 1774**

After the Boston Tea Party, clashes between colonists and British soldiers continued to grow.

The acts closed all routes in and out of Boston, including Boston Harbor. Trade would not resume until the East India Tea Company was repaid for its tea. Simple items, such as food and clothing, became difficult to find.

FAST FACTS

The Intolerable Acts had a side effect the British never intended. Patriots from around the colonies met to organize resistance against the British. Their meeting was called a convention. The convention later became known as the Continental Congress.

The colonists were further restricted by a military governor. The governor, General Thomas Gage, appointed all government officials. Town meetings and other gatherings were forbidden unless Gage called for them.

Gage had the power to move trials for British soldiers and officials to another colony or even to Great Britain. It was unlikely that witnesses to the crime would be able to cross the ocean to attend a court hearing. The colonists felt that British soldiers would be able to commit crimes and then escape, unpunished.

As part of the Intolerable Acts, the Quartering Act was rewritten. By 1774 soldiers were allowed to take over private homes if they needed a place to stay.

The colonists felt it was time to act. Their actions changed the history of the United States forever.

governor: a person who controlled a country or state during colonial times

CHAPTER 4

Fighting Back

Colonists began to take action against British laws. They formed protests, boycotted goods, and publicly voiced their opinions. They wanted to be heard by Great Britain, Parliament, and King George III.

British Soldiers Arrive in Boston (1768)

Following the Townshend Acts of 1767, Boston citizens boycotted British goods. The government became concerned for British-owned companies. Parliament also worried that colonists might destroy property or harm tax collectors. So they sent thousands of soldiers to the city.

The soldiers lived in a large camp on Boston Common. They were stationed in the city to prevent the soldiers from deserting. It made the colonists feel like they were in a prison. Many small fights took place between the soldiers and the colonists. Tensions continued to rise in the occupied town, eventually leading to the Boston Massacre.

The Boston Massacre (1770)

The troops' arrival sparked resentment throughout the colonies. Boston colonists felt like prisoners in their own town. The soldiers were constantly harassed and made to feel unwelcome. The constant friction between the two groups caused a series of small arguments.

By 1770 these arguments turned violent. Fights erupted between the soldiers and colonists. Crowds gathered around the commotion. Several brawls took place. Neither side wanted to back down.

British soldiers entering Boston made sure the colonists followed the new laws.

On March 5, 1770, a colonist named Edward Garrick began taunting a British soldier. The soldier used his gun to take a swing at Garrick. The colonists turned against the soldier. British Captain Samuel Preston noticed the crowd and ordered other soldiers to help.

The crowd grew. The Patriots threw snowballs, trash, and glass. Several charged the soldiers. One soldier hit a Patriot with the end of his gun. A colonist threw a hard object at a soldier. In the confusion, someone shouted fire. The British soldiers quickly unloaded their guns into the crowd. Moments later, Preston ordered them to stop.

Five colonists died in the shooting. Nine others were injured. Preston and eight soldiers were arrested and put on trial. Most soldiers were found not guilty of murder, but two were found guilty of manslaughter.

FAST FACTS

The guilty soldiers could have been executed for their crime. However, a British law allowed them to ask for special treatment. They were both given the lesser sentence of having the thumb on their right hands branded with a hot iron.

manslaughter: the unlawful killing of a person without intending to do so

After the trial, the British troops were moved out of Boston. By this time, however, the colonists believed the massacre was proof that the British were not afraid to use physical force.

The Bloody Massacre

A Patriot named Paul Revere drew a picture called "The Bloody Massacre." The drawing made it look like the soldiers were responsible for what happened in Boston. His piece of propaganda was printed throughout the colonies, fueling the colonists' anger toward Great Britain.

Patriots looking as if they were surprised by the attack

Captain Preston with a sword raised, as if he ordered his men to fire

No trash, snowballs, or debris on ground near soldiers

No colonists near the British, as if the colonists had not charged into the soldiers

The Boston Tea Party (1773)

In fall of 1773, three British ships arrived in Boston Harbor. They carried tea from the East India Tea Company. A tax was to be paid on the tea when it was unloaded.

The people of Boston refused to pay the tax. The tea sat on the ships in the harbor for two weeks. Patriot leaders petitioned the governor to have the tea returned to Britain. The governor refused.

About 50 members of the Sons of Liberty vowed that no tea would be unloaded. They dressed up as Indians and boarded the ships. The Patriots dumped more than 96,000 pounds (43,500 kilograms) of tea into the harbor.

The Sons of Liberty

The Sons of Liberty were Patriots who opposed British rule. The first group was formed in 1765 in Boston. Soon each colony had a branch. The Sons of Liberty led protests and mobs against tax collectors and soldiers. They wrote letters to the newspaper and posted signs calling for Patriots to fight. Their actions led to colonists taking a stand at the Boston Tea Party and Boston Massacre.

petition: a letter signed by many people asking leaders for a change

The tea was destroyed. King George III and Parliament were furious. They viewed the Tea Party as the highest insult to their authority. The cost of the wasted tea was estimated at more than $1.7 million in today's money. Parliament promised the East India Tea Company that Boston would pay for the damages.

It took about three hours for the colonists to dump all the tea into the harbor.

FAST FACTS

The Boston Tea Party is the most famous tea party, but not the only one. Virginia colonists broke into a warehouse and ruined the tea inside. A second tea party occurred in Boston a few weeks later. Colonists in Rhode Island actually set fire to a ship that carried tea.

CHAPTER 5

Preparing for War

By 1775 the colonists started to prepare for war. Years of unfair laws, heavy taxes, and the presence of soldiers had brought them to their breaking point. They began forming militias.

Patriot leaders Samuel Adams and John Hancock watched the proceedings from Lexington, Massachusetts. In nearby Concord, militias began stockpiling weapons and gunpowder.

King George III heard rumors of these stockpiles. He sent British soldiers to seize the weapons and capture Adams and Hancock.

Events Leading to the Revolution

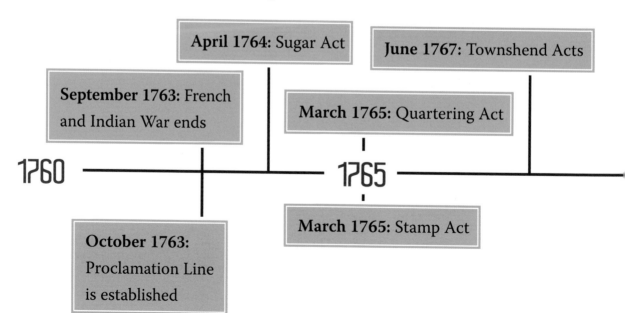

April 1764: Sugar Act

June 1767: Townshend Acts

September 1763: French and Indian War ends

March 1765: Quartering Act

1760

1765

October 1763: Proclamation Line is established

March 1765: Stamp Act

The colonists spread word that the British soldiers were marching from Boston. They prepared to block the soldiers from the town.

On April 19, 1775, the soldiers arrived in Lexington. They were blocked by a small group of militiamen. For a short time, the two sides stared each other down. Then a shot was fired. Nobody knows whose gun fired the shot. But after five minutes of shooting, eight colonists were dead.

The fight had allowed Adams and Hancock to escape. The soldiers continued on to Concord. Angry colonists gathered in the town and more shots were fired.

The Battles of Lexington and Concord were the first conflicts of the Revolutionary War. It would be eight long years before the last battle was fought. But the result would be American independence.

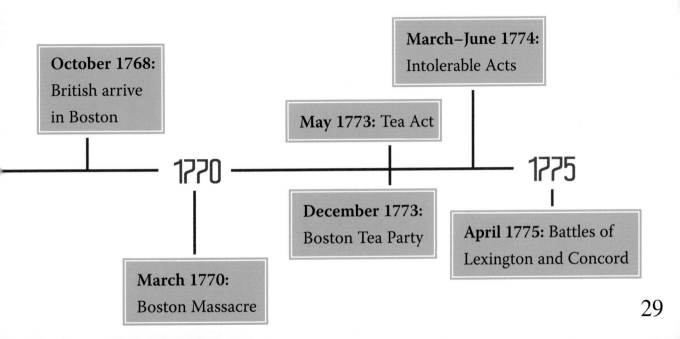

October 1768: British arrive in Boston

May 1773: Tea Act

March–June 1774: Intolerable Acts

1770

1775

March 1770: Boston Massacre

December 1773: Boston Tea Party

April 1775: Battles of Lexington and Concord

Glossary

boycott (BOY-kot)—to refuse to take part in something as a way of making a protest

confiscate (kon-FIS-kayt)—to take something by authority

debt (DET)—money that a person owes

governor (GUHV-urn-ur)—a person who controlled a country or state during colonial times

harass (ha-RASS)—to bother or annoy again and again

import (IM-port)—to bring goods into one country from another

manslaughter (MAN-slaw-ter)—the unlawful killing of a person without intending to do so

militia (muh-LISH-uh)—a group of citizens who are trained to fight, but who only serve in an emergency

parliament (PAR-luh-muhnt)—a group of people who make laws and run the government in some countries

petition (puh-TISH-uhn)—a letter signed by many people asking leaders for a change

propaganda (prop-uh-GAHN-duh)—information spread to try to influence the thinking of people; often not completely true or fair

repeal (ri-PEEL)—to officially cancel something, such as a law

smuggle (SMUHG-uhl)—to bring something or someone into or out of a country illegally

taunt (TAWNT)—to use words to try to make someone angry

Read More

Gondosch, Linda. *How Did Tea and Taxes Spark a Revolution?: And Other Questions about the Boston Tea Party.* Six Questions of American History. Minneapolis: Lerner Publications, 2011.

Raum, Elizabeth. *The Boston Massacre: An Interactive History Adventure.* You Choose Books. Mankato, Minn.: Capstone Press, 2009.

Samuels, Charlie. *Timeline of the Revolutionary War.* Americans at War. New York: Gareth Stevens Pub., 2012.

Internet Sites

FactHound offers a safe, fun way to find Internet sites related to this book. All of the sites on FactHound have been researched by our staff.

Here's all you do:

Visit *www.facthound.com*

Type in this code: 9781429684286

Check out projects, games and lots more at
www.capstonekids.com

Index